TRANSLATIONS

TRANSLATIONS

a collection of poems

DAVID LYLE JEFFREY

RESOURCE *Publications* • Eugene, Oregon

TRANSLATIONS
a collection of poems

Copyright © 2021 David Lyle Jeffrey. All rights reserved. Except for brief quotations in critical publications or reviews, no part of this book may be reproduced in any manner without prior written permission from the publisher. Write: Permissions, Wipf and Stock Publishers, 199 W. 8th Ave., Suite 3, Eugene, OR 97401.

Resource Publications
An Imprint of Wipf and Stock Publishers
199 W. 8th Ave., Suite 3
Eugene, OR 97401

www.wipfandstock.com

PAPERBACK ISBN: 978-1-7252-9030-3
HARDCOVER ISBN: 978-1-7252-9029-7
EBOOK ISBN: 978-1-7252-9031-0

01/21/21

*For my beloved Kate,
evermore and evermore . . .*

Contents

Foreword — xi
Acknowledgments — xiii

1 | Learning to Dance

On a Shore without Sight	3
Windwalk	4
Piano Bar	5
Explication: La lune	6
En bref	7
New Year's Morning in the Olympic Mountains	8
Windstorm	10
Amor to Psyche (when she quoted him poetry)	11
The Defense Replies...	12
Les Tres Riches Heures: Fevrier	14
Illuminated MS	16
Analogy	18
Songs in the Night	19
Refrain	20
A Wish	21
Proofreading	22
February 14, 2000	23
Hortus Conclusus	*24*
Goldstream	25
A Morning Meditation (Ps. 127:2)	26
An Anniversary Thanksgiving, for Kate	28
Island Beach	29

2 | Kith and Kin

Unposted, from Upper Canada	33
Eulogy, for my Mother	34
A Dream of Fishing	36
Nana's Metronome	38
Stanzas for Michael Josef	39
The River Road from Onslow	40
Adieu to an Old Saint at Dockside	42
Canoeing in the Barron River Canyon	43
Tempus Oportet	45
A Gift of Leaves, with Signature	46
Rainy Day Reader	47
To a Ballet Dancer	49
Domestic Chivalry	51
To a Bride	52
A Wedding Prayer	53
Migrations	54
Redeeming Time	55

3 | *Via Imperfectum*

Art	59
Collectors	60
Earthly Harmony, Heavenly Peace	61
The Last Illness of Deng Xiaoping	62
The Monkey-King Opera	63
Wan Li and the Two Empresses	64
Yanshan Hotel	65
Memories of an Old Colleague	67
Report of Two Witnesses	69
Red Lent	71
Irish Hat	72

Check-up	74
Masque	75
Richard and Margaret (ca. 1349 A.D.)	76
Midrash on Psalm 90	78
Nesi'a Tovah	*80*
Dasein und Widerspruch	*82*
Musings on an aphorism	84

4 | Prayers and Meditations

א Aleph	89
Biological Clocks of the Tidal Zone	90
Nighthawk River	92
ב Beit	94
Comfort in Imperfection	95
ג Gimel	96
Dèserted	98
Lent	99
Solitary Dove, Easter Morning	100
St. Barnabas Eve	102
Coin of the Realm	103
Madonna del Libro (Botticelli)	104
Child's Play and Painting	105
ד Dalit	107
Mary of Bethany, in Later Life	108
Musqueam Park	109
Nechamu	110
Semiotic	111
Future Perfect	113
Evensong: on Praying the Psalms	114

ix

Foreword

As one who has known the friendship of exemplary poets, Philip Larkin, Anthony Hecht, Richard Wilbur, and Micheal O'Siadhail among them, I certainly do not pretend to their guild. Rather, I am just a life-long reader of poetry who has found its languages to provide a helpful means of responding to people I do not always know well but have come to love. I have thus from time to time committed random acts of poetry as an acknowledgment that other lives, presently or from some distant past, have spoken to me in ways that move me to thoughtfulness and gratitude.

By "translations" in my title I refer not merely to spoken languages, but to the sense articulated by George Steiner in his *After Babel: Aspects of Language and Translation* (1975), in which "translation" also signifies the rich, complex, and perpetually incomplete process whereby we attempt to understand one another. One way we may do this is by offering an interpretation of some aspect of meaning in another person as we think we have glimpsed it. Poetry like this is not analytical, but merely part of an unfinished conversation in which only God could have the last word. The final section of this little collection draws on various personal stages in that less audible conversation.

September 15, 2020

Acknowledgments

Some of these poems first appeared in the following Canadian and American journals: "Musqueam Park," "Biological Clocks of the Tidal Zone," "Child's Play and Painting," and "*Les Tres Riches Heures: Fevrier*" in *Crux*; "Art" in the *Wascana Review*; "Nighthawk River" and "Windstorm" in *The Northward Journal*; "Piano Bar" in *Mythos*; "Songs in the Night" in *Whetstone*; "Masque" in *Canadian Poetry*; "*Madonna del Libro*," "Richard and Margaret," "Mary of Bethany," "Coin of the Realm," and "Transcendence and Philosophical Thought" (here titled "*Dasein und Widerspruch*") in the *St. Austin Review*; "Comfort in Imperfection" in *Modern Age*; "Unposted" and "Benediction" in *Local Culture*; "Future Perfect" appeared under the title "Anticipation" in *First Things*.

1

Learning to Dance

On a Shore without Sight

I'm waiting for you.
Though night bends low
droops wet on my neck in a yoke of rain
though the last light dims
and no music plays—
still this heart keeps time,
knowing to which soft tune it stirs,
offering limbs to be plucked like strings
in trust for a smile, for a word.

But in greying mists
when the slow light shapes,
beckons me reach for
a touch—a face—
and shadows hold no surprise,
then waking unlearns,
and heart under shoulders turns to mime
down long stone steps past the ebb of words,
as fixing my gaze beyond circling birds
I seek you, submerged, unheard.

Windwalk

Ashamed of my dreams, I wish the wind
would hide me.
Through old leaves and straw
Thoughts sail,
Torn loose in the twist of a gale,
Blown beyond pondering,
Dead in quandary.

As: who can think to know the wind?
Its coming, or where it goes?
Unanswerable questions, posed long ago,
Blow about my pathway still,
Toss me like a leaf,
Like a tuft of dry grass:
I can't make a sound.

I barely breathe this bitter cold;
can't bare my skin.
can't show a soul that falters.

So I walk with the wind
To hide me.
Ashamed of my dreams, I walk beyond sleep,
Deep in a brutal storm.

Piano Bar

For all I know these rifting thoughts
like notes from an old piano,
waves from the sea, or
chatter of birds in autumn flight
could scatter us both, plea bargaining.

Who speaks, self-seeking,
knowing each word reshapes the past,
admits that speech
betrays the facts? Yet these are words,
and I, a self, am pleading.

Our case, perhaps, is moot.

And yet, for all we know these falling notes
like tunes the old bartender hums
might sweep the counter clean,
chime off each glass, refract its glare
—recall us both, imagining.

Picture me then, as I
imagine you: still silent
in these empty arms;
I, to the rag-time music,
listening. . . .

Explication: La lune

J'ai vu la lune, la entendu
et comme toujours, d'un coeur rendu
le témoignage s'accorde, c'est toi
pour moi qui rends encore l'envoi
donne comme baiser la belle promesse,
touch la mémoire, soigne le tristesse
dis que je reste d'un pays perdu
loin de l'entreinte, ta douce sagesse.

Mais je rétourne enfin, chez vous,
et sur le monde ténèbres oublie
quand survolai terres inconnus
j'embracerai ton rêverie
en chaque rayon du clair decrû
je prie venir a ce qui j'ai crû.

En bref

J'ai vu la lune, tes mots reçus
et comme toujours ces aperçus
aussi je prends comme témoignage
et prie venir de ton visage
aussitôt que possible.

New Year's Morning in the Olympic Mountains

"The top of the world," you whispered
treading more closely on snowy slopes
where wraiths of the mist
like leopards' breath or altar smoke
drifted into our eyes.

Silence, and opening gaps
down spruce-lined steeps to worlds below
were wonders but not surprise.
We had been here before in dreams,
and the pure white light of winter's sleep
held a peace, we thought, for tortured times,
so we long looked up to these fabled hills
from another coast, yearning
past boundaries of wave and sky.

A summer then is winter now,
and my steps slow as seasons
their census count,
measure the mind's retreat:
climbed we so high just to pick our way,
unanswered down? That thin, cold air
sucked into hearts hard beating
grew still, unresolved in bodies' meeting—

for rest unrested, remaining to doubt
a downward trek through virgin trees.

Suddenly a doe, glistening
fearless and trusting to her aerie world:
did you see in her gaze some sign,
some secret of a higher will
or find there mere reflections,
shadowed pools where time stands still?

Signs portend signs. As ancient fables tell us,
mountains are for mortals moments,
not more. Returned to a flatter earth
each frames his speech, each makes a choice.
And these words too, we may forget, or
hearing again, let to life.
Only the heart could riddle a reason,
waken to act on love's command,
'ere each return to weighty burdens,
separate, shrouded, in an alien land.

Windstorm

(free transl. of BETEP, by Boris Pasternak)

"...and also because all creation is simpler than some of our crafty philosophers think." (Pasternak)

I have died. Yet your heart beats among the living.
And this groaning, shifting wind
unhallows the sacred grove, the woodland crosstrails,
bends the trees, in anguish strings their listing limbs

as one great chorus
this rhythmic forest
keens in a sad, strong dance,
abjures the distant stars

—it makes them rock,
rock as the hulls of sailboats in an unsafe harbor.

And still, the wind moves perfectly,
not by chance, nor in a senseless rage,
but so that in its desolation
it may find tunes
or even words
to woo from the night
a gentler light,
inscribe your sleep with lullabies.

Amor to Psyche (when she quoted him poetry)

"quam vasa figuli, quae sunt fragilia"

Since you insist, in faith,
then think us earthen vessels,
hoping to clasp, longing to be filled,
when spilled, each know our own fragility.

Yet in that logic, good my sage,
you ought comply
to own your image truly:
in maker's magic sculpture rise,
admit and blend a silver wine,
hold, shape—so mingle and refine,
that in these shards of love,
our clay,
rings magic maker's antic play
(sweet play,
and winged antinomies).

The Defense Replies...

"My beauty is in the eye of your beholding,"
you said, with a smile.
I protested; you thought it guile.
Beholden to you for a smile?
Ah yes,
and in that debate it won't be long
till hold and be
transverse
suborning me eternally—
to be and to have co-infinitive
free
yet suddenly me.

These eyes are always beholding
you
and softening, yielding;
seeing as you are,
so being
and holding you
so far as near
(whose smile all near implies)
that becoming you has hold of me.

Insouciant and lovely,
your beauty grows in the eye of my beholding,
knows well enough my plea:
that the love you live
in advocate eyes
holds a whole bright world to ransom,
captive to your smile,
beholden to you, unspoken,
for a long, long while.

Les Tres Riches Heures: Fevrier

Grow warm by this fire
Lady Blue:
outside, in snow the earth lies bound
—not you.

Under leaden sky and a trace of smoke
the woodsman's steady stroke
cleaves withered limbs from the frozen trees,
bare branches gathered on shivering knees
for hearths in town,
ride down on the back of an aged mule.

Here, all the while
in your whitened close
under rounded domes of woven reed
sleep summer bees.
While pigeons worry a spill of seed
new wine put in casks for your heart's delight
(though painted with ice)
shall warm in your breast
and with honey bright
waken your smile in the dancing light
for the moment of love's return.

I work to learn,
and over our huddled sheep have seen the thatch
torn through:
before gathering dark
I would make to their rest an old roof new.

Then, for warmth beyond wine,
repose more sublime,
more than meat and drink
turn home to you.

So be warm by the fire
Lady Blue:
the world outside in snow lies bound—
not you.

Illuminated MS

Down the smooth descending stair
your hair with each step falls
as fair as grass. Uneven echoes,
memories pass, as soft as dream
may trace a meadow, gold and green,
or skies so blue they turn to marble in the eye
remembering. Fiesole. Here evening stills the mind,
eyes turn; I take your hand again.

Far deeper slopes we walk than sleep,
where sculpted stones wind down to dark.
Stone steeps our doubt. In ancient bones
all hallows keep, in shadowed trust
wait sentinels—and dragons. Dust.
Columns of lanterns flicker, strake the wall.
Coolness. Caverns. Caves of the deep, I feel
you think, and of my hand's insistence, warm.

Yes—all of this in silence, prearranged.

The words we seek are locked in ink,
pages, poised from the ages
under glass. Believing words, I watch you
think: how beautiful her face, her hand.

And here, as in that court, we stand
attent like children; eyes bright, alive as those
whose frail, enameled gestures teach
that angels wait in wonder too,

are here as well composed. Released.
As drawn in gold and velvet leaf
you're brushed by the lightest stroke:
the artist's love seems painted true;
his figures apt as may ensue
in time for me or you. Transcribe us, then,
with patient eyes. Who early turned from love aside
could come to love this image too. Ascend.

Analogy

"neque. . .oculis non vidit"
Your dance my dreams could not devise:
Where senses strain, to stars aspire,
Pale moonlight yields to clay cool fire;
Light breaks from a dark surmise.
Then you, for healing anguished eyes
Re-choir the night with angel's voice;
The heart that harkens shall rejoice
And know itself beyond disguise.

Past thought, intent, above the mist,
One single word unveils the moon.
Arise, my love, and dance—come soon!
May starry nights portend that tryst,
Our ageless chase and restless ache
Assuage beside this silvered lake.

Songs in the Night

Ego dormio, et cor meum vigilat...
Yes, I sleep. But my heart is awake,
and even though drawn
in shadow's vale
where in memory's shade my body lies,
like a snow-white bloom on a field of green,
I would turn to a blush of light,
to the touch of my lover's hand
entwining cords in the rose-dawn light
pale reins in the April light.

Surge, amica mea, speciosa mea, et veni...
Awaken, my love, to life—
as opens the hand that touches the rose
so open your eyes:
arise to the world's first morning.
    Come loosen your long dim hair
    and ride,
    lissom as wings to the rising tide!
    And as beads of the dew in sundance flee
    past rivers of night in the azure light
    let hoofbeats run—
    let them run
    through silvered dreams to the golden sun,
    to jasper meadows by the golden sun.

Refrain

I'll take you away
one day:
the sun will rise,
the gulls wheel and cry,
there will be such a light in the sky!

A Wish

I want to trace your life
in words as whole and true

as soft as perfect pearls of dew
as new

and yet as old as love
and rhyme

and still as stone
shall harbor time.

Proofreading

There's a misprint in your hair;
A strand detached is proof enough
Your grace was mine
(as well as theirs) to share.

Good that your face is fair,
Soft and becalmed as wax.
They'll read no trace of my design
Though I retouched that smile you wear.

February 14, 2000

Snow swirls round our porch-yard door,
the sky is wound in whitening sheets
of snittering, biting, airborne ice.
A saint of love might find it nice
To stay with you in bed.

Alas for love like Valentine's
our season's not a tropic choice
and winter's habits culture vice.
Red socks and knickers must suffice
to keep you warm instead.

Hortus Conclusus

Varied hues, all shapes, beautiful glades
in dappled light, leafy canopies,
ivy twining on a latticed frame,
coleus, burgundy and green, violets
of all shades, carpet, entwined
      embrace.

All these things pretexts are for poetry.
Butterflies and birdsong play a part.

Forgotten longings come to mind
when seeing's lost in wonder.
Desires unvoiced upstart the heart.
If lips or fingers move,
words cease, give way to touch—
      in gardener's hands, a lover's face.

Goldstream

Along the pebbled banks of that far river
aspens shimmer, refract the morning light;
a scattering of gems on trilling waters
gleams, gold-flecked, jade green, granite streaked.

It will be the same and not the same.
Each deep pool hoarding its silver trout,
but not the same trout. Each raven's croak
canny, alike, but not such somber omen.

Here, close by a limestone lake, are hints
of that penumbral glade where once we walked,
talked, pressed each to each our thudding hearts,
till turning back, reluctant, gravel scrunching under feet.

It is comfort now to think of you then,
Eyes blue as the sky, lips like petals, heaven.

A Morning Meditation (Ps. 127:2)

The haze which cloudy dawn dispels,
More mist than light,
Suffuses now your pillowed face.
I, first awake, desire
—yet hesitate.

To know your blissful, gentle grace
Yet standing bless your rest is meet;
Extend your dreaming into day.

Outside trees with birdsong swell;
Doves weep, and blousy geese
Wing down to glide along the creek.

Our farmyard stirs: maternal mood
And marriages throng up in every nook
—and still you sleep!

How gently might I rouse you, lass—
Commute this throbbing pulse
To deeper dreams you keep,
And fain would nigh those parted lips
To touch or kiss,
But wistful, let you slumber on
Through clouds of down past daybreak.

Such peace I will not breach,
Though gladly would I wake your love
Who here as gladly bless your sleep.

An Anniversary Thanksgiving, for Kate

"Perfect love casts out fear." (1 John 4:18)

Can it now be so long?
Years slip by like months
at best; each day with you
mere moments, like angel songs.

Most perfect joys are brief—
we seek their repetition;
the rhythms of joined life
springing evergreen in bud and leaf.

Twelve troubled years before you came,
then twenty more before I saw your eyes,
still ten again before I knew
how your ripe love could drop like rain

upon my arid earth: those years
were long and parched—
but now their length's forgotten.
Love conquers time; love slaked my thirsty fears.

Island Beach

For Katherine at Christmastide

Along soft, slow curves of an island beach
where sand lies smooth on the tidal ebb
as fine gold carpet, children play,
lost to the world. We watch.

Couples walk their frisking dogs;
a terrier bounds happily by
fetching a ball, redundant, antic joy.
And all the while the tide ebbs out, itself
redundantly to come again, predictably,
as long as time and tide keep count.

For someone on the beach perhaps
this tide shall be the last egress;
in glistening sand and water
mark one last reckon with creation's clock,
its muffled chime. In the beauty
of the evening time for some shall cease,
the cosmic dance, play and begetting,
shall, like hearts, stand still.

Yet this is not the end of it—
The scape escapes all reckoning.

In some far universe, galaxies, perhaps, apart
(or barest nanometers, to speculation not diaphanous),
another strand of molecules, billions more,
stretch and shape another shore and sea.

If there small children play, dog's sport,
or those who feel time's metric watch,
we cannot know; can only guess.
Yet stand we here as one, contend with none,
in our brief scene content; in rolling, steady waves
still hear the timeless angels' song.

2

Kith and Kin

Unposted, from Upper Canada

Tonight at dusk the fields are purple;
clover, second-cut, gone to bloom
in the intermittent rain. It sweeps in mottled waves
up and down, as heather might
in old Scotland.

We keep no sheep to feed the wolves,
but on long slopes in slanting light
I see the shapes of cattle grazing,
calves a-suckle, as at eve they might
in another glen.

Kinfolk rest,
the long day's work is done.
A chorded rhythm strikes and becks;
a lilt of singing over strings
comes to me soft on fragrant air.

Dew gathers on roses by our door.
I light a candle, blow the match,
and twice pour amber from the flask.
A settled peace, a goodly thing,
Comes on with sundown, love's warm wing.

Eulogy, for my Mother

Far from the sea, over glistening loam
gulls follow the plough; small birds flock,
like seedcast spread and fall in the evening sky.
The air is crisp, smart with the smell of apples,
hints of frost. Eyes wait upon crimson,
on gold-dappled, pine-braced slopes
lifting the hills in glory
above the fertile fields.

These are the latter blooms,
their fruitful season a tender touch
maturity lays on every vista, each in its way and time.
Once all things green as the first bud strove
unripe, slight as sap in a bucket.
Then came daisies, dancing,
berryripe lips, supple with laughter
as all creation brought forth its young.

Who now could not, as then, rejoice?
When days shorten, shadows stretch
sharp in the autumn light, wise eyes take everything in;
chrysanthemums by the porch
sense the great gathering hymn, that glad thanksgiving.

Quiet, prayerful, heart's collected thought
now knows what the birds know, winging:
all this is planting—God's.
All beauty shall return to him.

A Dream of Fishing

*for my father, who took his Sunday School class fishing
one Saturday in 1948, and included me*

Some acts of affection in an ordinary life
seem slight and yet suffice.
Love is a potent bait, an element
so strong we trace its scent miles hence, far
down the river poured through memory.

Such is my remembering of you:
a simple act of inclusion in a time of loss,
acceptance into a fellowship—or so I thought—
for a confused and grieving boy,
one place in a rented boat.

Lightest of all, I perched on the bow,
my fish-line baited with worms.
The older boys trolled to the side,
while you, your red and white spinner astern,
manned the motor and whistled a tuneless song.

At noon you caught the first fish,
and when its glistening, gray-green side
and toothy head swung to the net
I rejoiced at such providence
and let my hand trail in the wake.

The water flowed cool and fresh through my fingers;
I lifted my hand and looked close
as if to see for the first time.
In the afternoon sun I lay on the bow,
head over, seeking more glimpses of life.

That night I slept better, and dreamed
I was again a fisherman's boy,
and when dark, unanswered thoughts returned,
pressing me down to the deck,
I put head, not hand, in the water.

Clear water can be its own reward.
At once I felt darkness washing away
back under the boat, a grey cloud
staining the prop-wash. My head snapped up,
escaping the cloud. I saw your rearward gaze.

Down the long years I have dreamed
this memory many times;
each time awoke released, then slept,
holding that upside-down image in my mind:
you, hand on the tiller, whistling your tuneless song.

Nana's Metronome

"For every drop of rain that falls
A flower grows." So believed my father's mum
who sang it mournfully,
played out her tuneful sadness
on a Baldwin upright, slightly flat.

Tears filled her vacant eyes,
glistened as she played and sang
where no rose bloomed. Only
the fading petalled pattern of her dress
and cloying scent of English talc
lent fancy to her formless faith.

Yet she was kind. Her crystal bowls
of Scotch mints and toffee soothed
what, for a child, her music missed.
And steady in the sleepless dark
I heard the simple measure,
tick and tock,
grandfather's clock in the empty hall.

Stanzas for Michael Josef

born January 1, 1977

Crouched at the casement of the year
life within life, poised under shroud,
you swam like a nova into our sphere,
slipped silently, out of the night
from months of slumbering, formless cloud
to be definite, as keen as light.

Ferreting down to outstretched hands
and reaching out, you struggled free;
how could you guess what love demands,
faith needs? More than you know comes new
to these close and shuttling hearts; on her knee
at rest dreams more than a wish come true.

Your life and the year we gladly praise,
marking the cross of tales untold.
When words and the moment touch, lips raise
old songs to praise our Father's will;
they tell that time shall yet stand still,
the light remake, our songs rephrase.

The River Road from Onslow

for my parents, at Montebello, on the sixtieth anniversary of their marriage, June 1, 2000

Still that old road, now smoothed of care,
rolls over and down the ageless hills;
past sentinel pines the wild plum spills
bright warblers into the morning air.

By pastures fair the swallows climb
above where quiet cattle graze;
at the crest of a hill two cyclists gaze
out where the river runs to rhyme.

'Tis fine to find in familiar parts
such ready space to share a dream;
as geese wing down to their chosen stream,
good purpose, hope in expectant hearts.

Of all fine arts love bears the crown,
its memories swell the flow of time;
each creek flows in, broadens the line
enriches more, obtains renown.

Not songs and cheerful mirth alone,
but tears, new hope, and life again;
each kindred grief, each joy's refrain,
deepens trust, still turning home.

One day in June the river glides in,
most calm by these shores of all.
Two cyclists ride up to a banquet hall,
are merrily met by kith and kin.

Within and without great cheer they raise
(from far and wide they've come)
to honor a journey sought and won
through to a feast of fitting praise.

For you of blessèd, early choice,
of future blessings sponsors still;
for you our parents, one in will,
we each are thankful, each rejoice.

Adieu to an Old Saint at Dockside

for Dorothy, Port Angeles, Nov. 12, 1996

Softness. Though brittle the shell
of emptied bone, sclerotic hardening,
loosened flesh and frail, transparent skin,
a spirit sweet as morning's dove
still murmurs clear her mother's love.

I came to hold her hand,
unspell my trove of thankful debt,
to say a last farewell.
She, smiling, did not scorn my tears,
but wanted more confessed.

For yet another's need she sought,
another's life to grace, fulfil
with benedictions wrought in trust
and expectations of release;
my duty now to keep her peace.

At length we kissed and turned our eyes,
sent on our separate ebbing ways,
my rough bark set fresh afloat,
hers on a last home slip and glide,
glistening, light on an even tide.

Canoeing in the Barron River Canyon

for Bruce

Read, my son, for shadows grow long
Across this page, even as I write.
Already wise and skilled in dreams,
You will know what this means.
        Swift rivers rush down to dark,
And vessels of men prove weak. Seep.
Bleeding barques with cargoes of ink
Swirl down to their last, unbidden deep.

Not all these things can be turned with a song.
Not I, nor the One who writes the world,
Spinning his line through the darkling stream,
Expect you to pretend it.
        Yet remember the ark,
The forty days, the rainbowed years,
And all the time this river flowed,
Sweeping past all rocks and fears.

Some that paddle knew never a tune,
Did not in the wistful woodnotes mark
The descant pibroch thrill they heard:
Tomorrow, too, shall pass. You hark.

So look to these hills, though stark;
Draw strength from the gentle morning breeze
And lift your blade with a joyful heart,
Renewing each stroke from anchored knees.

Tempus Oportet

for Bruce

Each strike of the old wall clock
jars, grates at a scarred nerve,
marks under skin the unwound hours.

The chime counts oddly, off by seven—
to the eye four, ear eleven, as in York
where I bought it when the lad was six

—already old. "A century of bartered memories,
Guv. Ten quid." I mind it better now,
that tinny note, the regulatory click
it brought to uneasy rooms
till stopped, boxed for years
in a voiceless tomb.

Here now on a distant shore, surprised by light,
the old brass pendulum swings again,
released, as if an English spring
renewed in the lad—a man now strong—
its steady, fruitful reason.

A Gift of Leaves, with Signature

for Kirstin

To gift or not to gift: the artist's question.
For giving is the crux; to understand a finer art,
loving another life.
To ask what she would like
is like to dream her, dreaming home;
her heart 'is like', more apt
to speak in her the kingdom of her love.
It reigns where kindness beggars present, time or place.

What she wants, you see
is space to have the lost brought back,
their ancient rune or faded page reviewed
—construed in love—
as leaves of the wistful summer,
red stained now and gold,
are harvested in hope of winter light.

There, where once stilled voices still can murmur
in a school-girl's ear
they gather—rustling leaves,
bouquets and scatterings of breath and breeze.
And she is there,
hers the ears to hear, the seeing eyes,
the deep, unhardened heart
which garners, kisses, keeps.

Rainy Day Reader

for Kirstin

The face at the window, speckled with rain,
freckled, fair and unashamed,
indwells another book. Curled in a cove,
glass and drape, she dreams another life.

All sunlight there is dappled, sheen;
all fledgling birds together sing.
Over the hills on beautiful feet
her hero, softly, bears his rose.

No shadow there of change,
no travail with remorse,
light falls upon a well-marked trail,
the way is blazed by ancient trust.

No night there falls bereft of hope,
nor bitter morn to follow tears.
Her prince will surely find her yet,
and gladly know her sweet repose.

There faithful love sleeps sound and safe,
awakes to purest touch,
and love rewarded in such kind
each loss excises, cancels doubt.

Under my rain-soaked tree I stay
To pray a splendid denouement:
bells a-ringing, clear songs winging—
golden, like her favorite book.

To a Ballet Dancer

for Adrienne

A father could wish one word would hold you
suspended, thus, on a point of flight;
tiptoe, teetered on a brink
where every moment tilts the light
unbending.

You skip, wee dancer, in the garden,
winking at my art
like some wood-sprite from the mountain,
elven image in my heart
—still dance!

Now I see *your* art is changes,
quick feet that touch, so spry
the hummingbirds bedazzled gasp
and circling seabirds, reeling, cry
their lack of compass.

Yours is the play of instant odds,
so making each step a sudden game,
escaping the craft of dragons dark
by teasing the monster, changing its name
to 'mister.'

My wish aims at giants over the wall,
Sly, shaping their ploys in smooth disguise,
hence, swift as you are on twinkling feet,
your quickness then with ears and eyes
I pray for.

Yet skip, lithe dancer, in the garden now,
winking at this heart,
like a wood-sprite from the mountain,
elven image of my art—
dance on!

Your art is life.

Domestic Chivalry

for Adrienne

Her beauty now by a window framed,
face to a pane, mists the glass.
She gazes out, then down; eyes trained
upon an open field of winter grass
      where two small lads, each armed with a bow,
shoot arrows at targets taped on a box.
All eyes are focused—above and below—
but hers more searching, keen as a fox.

These are her children, apples of her eye,
her own fixed aim as their arrows sail by.
Ensconced in this moment, each plays an old part,
till time shall be memory, taken to heart.
      When whooping with glee, her archers come in,
      they'll bring some new trophies, their princess to win.

To a Bride

for Kristina

For baby's breath and roses
In your hands, enfolding
An intent upon embrace
In time's ripe fullness—fitting.

And petals gathered bloom
Amidst your hair, crowning
The sweetness of your face,
Your smile's shy welcome—greeting.

Ah, the silken swish
Of taffeta and lace, stepping
Out in delicate pace
To love's true altar—keeping

Your tryst with gladness,
Bearing your troth about you like a song.

A Wedding Prayer

for Gideon and Anne

Behold, the bride and groom are come
to festive tables, gathered friends.
Here all make merry; daughter, son,
joined now to sacramental ends,
are blest in meeting, blessed as one.

We who share this welcome day,
their joy, their vows, their trust,
do bless ourselves, here with them pray
that theirs shall be a life so just
as Love shall honor, come what may.

So may, good Lord, their hours be filled
with kindness, wisdom, mirth and song;
may they through labors, cares distilled,
live out their troth both deep and strong,
return this day, each year, as thrilled.

And that their zest for life attune
to grand occasions such as this,
we ask, good Lord, one further boon:
a few wee bairns, born of bliss,
in bounteous love affirmed—and soon!

Migrations

for Joshua

A bird in flight is a fearless thing,
        Delicate, light, yet strong;
Its heart beats sure in an easy yoke,
        Lorica lifted, swifting along
On wings of feathers, streams of song.

So, windward from our homeward hearts,
        Makes westward now each fading day,
Till that called east, our natal place,
        Lies lost in darkness, far away,
Bequeathed to others as we pray.

Though migrating souls are tossed
        By many a bruising gale,
The westering light which draws us on
        Keeps minds on One who set the sail:
No stormy night shall long prevail.

Who follows stars—their course is changed:
        Transformed by glory, Luna's face
Shines back its radiant beams,
        Ensures this way Apollo's race
Speeds on in wonder, love and grace.

Redeeming Time

a Scottish air, for Jill, on her 60th birthday

Sure, time and tide will have their way;
Some features of our coastline change.
Despite what cheerful friends may say,
Our boats want paint, have briefer range.

Before us spread, the clouded sky
Hides storms or calm beyond our ken.
Yet let not fear, nor sea-bird cry
Suppress our will to launch again.

We put each day our crafts to sea,
To surge and swell let out our sail,
Again to seek where love may be
And pray fair winds may thence prevail.

So till that last long tide runs out,
Keep well your course, allay each doubt.

3

Via Imperfectum

Art

"And when I was a child,"
she said,
"I dreamed that God sat, smiling,
in a glass-box office
halfway up the sky,
in his dark red shirt and
beige felt hat
all middle-aged and friendly.

"I used to fly there
and he would talk to me
nicely
though what he actually said has slipped away.
I remember just that his name was Art
and later thought that he must have been
the one to whom we prayed in school
'Our Father who Art in Heaven.'"

Then she laughed aloud as she spoke that name
and turned to herself
and cried.

Collectors

They gather round a table, oddly spread,
on which an old and tattered tome
is laid, leaves open, binding cracked
so far as might allow it to be read.

These are such as one might pass
not seeing, garb and visage drab,
grey like the page on which they look,
and frail. One reads, "All flesh is grass."

A dozen eyes peer down, their glasses glint like beads.
The page beneath them shadows, "but,"
their lector turns the leaf: ". . . the word of God
forever stands." He adds, "or so it reads."

His almost inadvertent gloss is shy.
"The text is not so old as that,"
one jokes. The reader now, though mute,
remembers more, and wonders why

his colleagues, men of letters, seldom took
much time to read or contemplate this book.

过去

Earthly Harmony, Heavenly Peace

"Heaven is my Father and Earth is my Mother, and even such a small creature as I find an intimate place in their midst."

(Chang Tsai)

Supposing this earth—our Mother—
her dank, nutritious humus curved
around each upward thrust
of sprout, bud, bloom, seed
that later slips back in as dust;

imagine then the Father,
the infinitesimal seed
wound down with soft rain,
the morning sun, all clouds afloat
on warm winds once again.

现在

The Last Illness of Deng Xiaoping

Somewhere in this windswept, ochred maze
an old man sleeps, about to die
—or dead already, molders under wax.
Somewhere close the managers of thought
compose a scene to serve.

Outside the poplars bend and sway.
The square is nearly bare.
An unseen orchestra thrice has played
its somber march, then ceased.
The curtains billow and whip.
Strong wind in the leaves portends a rain
but blows deceit: this parched Mongolian air
freights only dust.

Cab-horns, two or three. A woman's voice
on loudspeakers, hailing the streets
a block or so beyond and always out of sight.
More noise of traffic further off.
Such are the mysteries of each fragile day;
each hints disclosures, indifferent
bids to postpone, delay.

过去, 现在

The Monkey-King Opera

With each flip and dazzling technicolor leap
the Monkey-King subdues to blur
another troubling thought.
The monsters that assail his path
—brigands, gods and spirits dark—
now trip the golden light,
their dread forgotten.
I pour my tea, its jasmine cup
spectral against the night beyond the stage.
The acrobat's riposte is braver mockery
than I might risk:
he beats them down with a laugh.

For the whole of his work is primed for mirth,
the skein of the operatic plot
a prance through rituals of comic relief
that might not end so merrily.
Thus strangely sad, I ponder still his pilgrim quest,
those true Scriptures yet unread
whose promise pricked, whose lure and beckon
drew his fabled journey on, brimming with hope,
for thoughts inarticulate, a bright articulation.

过去

Wan Li and the Two Empresses

"When the triple threes are complete, the Dao returns to its roots." (Wu Cheng' en)

Lace cypress boughs here sway
over a stone-wrought cobbled way.
Rounding old Ming's encrypted clay,
persimmons ripen once again.

Within, the fruit is dry as dust.
Down vaulted steps in blackened trust
rich coffins came, as slow they must,
heavy with jade and fame.

What should they cry, whose darkness falls
within such close, constricting walls?
What comfort silk when demons crawl
through drug-spun gauze and pain?

That gold and majesty are vain;
that imperial maggots feed on shame.

现在

Yanshan Hotel

From such unreal heights a watcher misconceives,
misjudging both distance and depth.
The air sweeps cool, scatters its light
upon sifting mist and dust. Leaves scatter:
the poplars below are stripped, as I watch,
of the mantle which for decent months
adorned the street below,
masking the usual deformities.

From here the choired and spectral dancers
move like leaves in muted ranks
and weaving throngs of cyclists, lorries, cars
all seem penumbral, images on a somber screen.
The ritual music stops. I close my window, snap,
dress quietly in modest clothes,
then descend to meet you by the door.
My focus shifts.

You are here, after all, satchel in hand.
We meet, greet and take a table.
Coffee for two. The waiter disappears
and then we lift our eyes to look:
eyes into eyes at risk. Again.
The slant and hue each grow distinct.

The lines in faces blossom, each unique.
Your quiet gaze is deeper than I thought.

过去, 现在

Memories of an Old Colleague

Walking around the Nameless Lake
under the drooping flowered trees
and pausing by the jasmined groves
you might never think of it now.

Birds now flit from branch to branch.
Close to the petalled water students sit
like lovers anywhere, paired,
or singly read in the tranquil shade.

Beyond this island, articulated
tiles, classical Qing,
break the tree tops; the high pagoda
crowns an idyll, so to speak.

Yet here on this very green
camped youthful hordes
their thousand screaming faces
chanting for old professors' blood.

"Bourgeous capitalist-roaders!"
was the universal charge.
Here frail old men and women
crouched in terror before the hurling dung.

Many did not survive. Others
somehow, up to their thighs in mud,
consumed with snail-fever,
clung to their sanity by reciting poems.

Some only later sickened and slowly died.
The botanist—our old professor—
was bricked up under stairs
and fed occasionally through the steps.

It took him six weeks to sink
and die in his own excrement.
His widow still lives, not far away,
embroidering handkerchiefs. She will not speak.

Over there we were forced
to cut down his peach trees,
plant cabbages, thus know peasant work.
That earth was not good for cabbages.

Look how the weeping willows move
so lightly in the wind. And sweet
is the scent of these forget-me-nots.
One might never think of it now.

现在

Report of Two Witnesses

Like everyone else they climbed aboard
the bus where it stopped at Xidan.
The workers were tired, heading home.
But the two old women, peasant-dressed,
side by side, began to sing.

Their song was, well, melodious—
if not familiar to our ears, at least
we saw their pleasure in singing.
We listened, uneasy, then curious
as words betrayed the origin of their song.
Not accents of Shandong or Hebei;
these were hymns of the Little Flock.
They sang of a shepherd, a Lamb
once slain for the sake of other lambs.

There was more. After two such songs
the women got up, with toothless smiles
passed out leaflets with sentences from their Book
to everyone on board. We refused.
When a young soldier asked them why,
they came beside him and for several blocks
talked eagerly of their Jesu as though
his was the only love the world had ever known,

as if the soldier were a little child
and they were both his dying mother
getting in their last words.

At Dongdan market they as suddenly bid farewell,
got off and slipped into the teeming crowds.
We think they might have gone to another bus.
But from whence they came,
or whither like wind they went,
we cannot tell.

现在

Red Lent

Some have chosen to forget
the rain-drenched open trucks,
demonstrations, denunciations,
character posters, struggle sessions,
obligatory train trips
made so the red might spread;
on bourgeois beaten down
between the cars,
belts swung hard, buckles of brass,
more brutal than knuckles.
Even I had almost forgotten
their screams half-muted in the clatter,
the battered bodies, dragged off by a boy
at every station.
I knew that boy,
and knew him again, fifty years beyond,
well up the tracks where, seeing me,
he could then remember too,
and privately, at a party, confess.

Irish Hat

Before we left that night
I had a dream.

We were rambling, you and I
And you were laughing
For sweet air, the sun
And the trees dancing.

I wore that hat you gave me
And climbed so high
The birds gave up.

We fairly leapt across the valley,
Moving up the rim
Till far behind the hard green water curled
Like twine in the gap below.

But near the top came a change:
Like the shaft of an arrow
Cold and bright,
Like a hole in my heart
The wind slipped in.
Suddenly my head was light
And that old hat went floating off—
Out like a hawk, and down.

And then, no matter how I waved
Or tried to call it back
It just fell on
Into the river's twist and turn
Like a lost brown leaf
It dropped.

Yes, friend,
That grand old Irish tweed
Went off like smoke
And I awoke, all memories drifting.

Check-up

"The biological clock is ticking,"
said the doctor, voice flat—
like that mechanic this morning, surveying her tires,
oil dripping from her Audi perched on the rack.
Herself more racked, and now discalced,
resenting intrusions, longing to be away,
or find some way to rewind the clock, like stale film,
serially exposed and (well she knew it) largely spent.

"Life is not a loom," her mother said;
mistakes in the warp one hardly unweaves,
but not in the woof, she meant.
Some scars go deeper than a speculum cleaves.

The hourglass on her office shelf,
bought for its charm (and feminine shape),
now loomed in her mind: *tempus fugit.*
That cliché at its base she took then
as a prompt: "make hay while the sun shines,"
like, "*carpe diem,* baby—seize the day."
Such was the impulse of her forthright mind,
impatient for kicks after closing time.

Masque

*"What in the World most fair appears,
Yea, even Laughter, turns to Tears."*

(Andrew Marvell)

Antimony unbidden, laughter, pain,
Gathers, glimmers in fugitive eyes
though brows, still ardent, arch
and coiffed hair swirls, immaculate.

When beauty hopes for refuge
sheer verve and sparkled glance,
deflect enquiry, shield a secret wound,
though one who seeks may find it.

Poise and counterpoise enfoil,
unweave to spin the dancer out
through yearning into risk—
stardust to night, inviolate.

Should tempo alter, light refract,
a child might see the tears held back.

Richard and Margaret (ca. 1349 A.D.)

". . .and when I die, disease shall not have been the cause."

(Richard Rolle, Melos Amoris)

Far from him. That was the worst of it.
Her anguished doubts about her calling
wrung holy incantations, rote, in the Roman tongue;
yet sacred song did not console her yearnings long.

When the other came fierce upon her,
each epileptic seizure, an embrace of death,
choked her mute in spasms; the ghastly grip
in which she froze terrified the older nuns.

They called for him then, past midnight,
her comforter and teacher, and he came
to find her *in extremis;* was admitted to her cell.
She lay contorted, stiff on the stone floor.

He raised and held her close.

Time passed. Unimaginably, at prime
she shuddered, cried aloud: "*Gloria tibi, Domine!*"
and came to life. Surprised by the old familiar face,
weeping, she leant her head against his shoulder

like a child. At length he spoke in soft, slow words:
"Even had you been the devil, I would have held you."
"Never again," he said before he left,
shall you have such an attack."
But seven years on she did, and he was then remote.

When they went for him, to Hampole,
they found him dead; at the very hour of her convulsions
his own heart stopped. She heard; her seizures came no more.
Her tongue released, she measured out her days in English song.

Midrash on Psalm 90

*A Maskil concerning the General Decrepitude,
for Stanley Hersh*

"For everything there is a time,
a season," quoth Qoholeth.
To such a text none can object
nor kvetch, though
after all the scroll of years,
the medley of satisfactions, tears
and undeserved general happiness,
the *mushel* seems superfluous.

But since it's in Ecclesiastes,
canonical, it gets repeated, and
authority so familiar breeds irony.
Sure enough, life happens as it will.
In time one becomes a cliché.
(At my age, I am less good than ever at subtle.
I don't even detect my own puns;
my jokes are best when accidental.)

Three-score and ten, according to Moses,
is a good measure, all things considered,
and if by reason of strength a bit more
is pressed into our cup, we should beware:
the surplus may give hiccups,

gas, dozy occlusions, weird parables.
We twitch as much as sleep at night,
awaken groggy, confused by light.

Nesi'a Tovah

for Stanley Hersh

כִּי טוֹב־יוֹם בַּחֲצֵרֶיךָ, מֵאָלֶף:

As strangers in a strange land,
we wander not so much as wonder
why we were given no map.

Only this story, a mental burr,
nostalgia for what we can name,
remember as words, but not know

as we are known by another
whose land this really is,
whose fair city we but dream,

hearing it rumored in an alien tongue
that eye has not seen nor ear heard
what banquet has been prepared

for unexpected guests in that far country,
feasting, blessing, bread that comes
sweet but unbroken, wine poured out,

and on our lips an unfamiliar song,
one we could not learn here,
a song our hearts could not have known,
gives words our tongue could not have spoken.

Dasein und Widerspruch

(notes on a conversation with three young philosophers)

Heidegger's mesmeric, incantatory prose
wrought thick facsimiles for transcendence;
like Wagner with sacred anthem's art, confused
Der Volk. *Gedenken ist Gedanken*[1] only sounds religious.

All such alchemy has this thin excuse:
to be thankful one can think at all
is minimal premise to a slim philosophy,
yet never, contra Descartes, thought identity.[2]

Scripture recommends thus fear of the Lord
as prolegomena to any future metaphysics.[3]
For reflection so begun, the German glib equation fails:
thinking and thanking are *not* the same,
but a reciprocity of mystery, call and response.[4]
Meditation and prayer may be harmonic,
as Augustine confessed, but need both I and Thou, attuned.[5]

---

1. *Thinking is Thanking*
2. Descartes' *cogito ergo sum* is finally an identification of the thinking self as the actual subject of reflection.
3. Immanuel Kant, *Prolegomena to Any Future Metaphysics*, 1783.
4. Cf. Psalm 1:2.
5. I.e., the dialogic construction of his *Confessions*.

These are not "two registers of the same voice";
Conrad more darkly saw the solipsism.[6]

A sceptic might as well assert:
thinking may be thankful if
—and only if—
there is a transcendent Other
listening, hearing when one prays.

This primal insight, absent worship, comes undone.
Knowledge of itself resists no clever charm,
nor seduction when desire burns, confused.
Consider Hannah: so intelligent, so duped.[7]
Into the subtle web fall even such,
logic lost to rhetorical spin,
succumbing softly, incense in their ears,
scarcely conceiving the hissing of the gas.

---

6. The reference is to the narrator's acerbic comment on the relationship of the self-absorbed lovers in his novel *Lord Jim*.

7. Hannah Arendt, author of *Men in Dark Times*, etc, was a graduate student and lover of Martin Heidegger, who became a prominent Nazi sympathizer.

Musings on an aphorism

Amor ipse intellectus est...

for L.N.

Love is the first word. By some blithe mystery it just slips in,
unobtrusively as slender feet in wool socks, softly
treading a tile floor. Enters: a presence, at first almost
imperceptible, yet definite as fresh air breathed
or lambent light slanting suddenly into the room.
Eyes lift from the page, behold a cherished face.
Nearby shelves of ferruled leather tomes retract.
Old titles slip from focus, glimmer, stardust cast,
and thus love bids, with such a subtle beck and call,
that heart kens well before mind reacts.

Learning love is next; its play a careful tact
set forth, a teaching. Love's then an art, disposing will,
perforce bestirring conscious thought with mindful check.
Yet fond desire enables more. In myriad languages love
outs; seeks speech, first making way by touch,
attention to the slightest hint, light whimsy in a glance,
striving by all sweet means to court, to bless,
learning by gift the promised part. Love learns by heart.
Learning in love perfects unspoken understanding;
grateful, protective, by thoughtful practice love refines.

Itself is notwithstanding, therefore grace. Embraced in faith,
in trust despite the odds, is patient to be proved,
attentive to another's inner quirk or pain.
Step by step, 'beloved' discloses what love means.
Then truths within and stars above concur.
Later, when hearth's last flames decline,
eyes close upon the heart-held face;
ears hear in chambered choirs one sweet voice,
soft as a footfall—or, in peals of recollected laughter,
guileless exclamations of a blameless joy.

4

Prayers and Meditations

א Aleph

That Voice: "Let there be light."

So, in ten thousand places,
God's quick eye, like an artist's brush
dapples the ground; sunlight and shadow
gather tones. Each hue

spangled, spired, slips down in prisms,
trilliums' enrapturing, shaping leaves
like hands and eyes enjoined,
embracing their love of light.

And all of this was done
        before one word was sung—
                before the sound of that Voice had passed away.

Biological Clocks of the Tidal Zone

"In the sands between the tide marks on the north shore of Cape Cod live a microscopic golden brown algae, the diatom hantschia virgata. . . . During each day-time low tide the tiny motile organism glides up through the interstices between the grains of the sand to the surface. There it remains through the ebb tide, its photosynthetic machinery bathed in sunlight. In mid-summer the diatoms are so abundant that in spite of their microscopic size they form a prominent brown carpet over the beach. Moments before they are inundated by the returning tide they move down into the comparative safety of the sand. . . . It seems that within the [single cell] plants there is a biological clock that directs the temporal aspects of their lives." (Scientific American, Feb. 1975, p. 70).

Countless preterient dots of green
blown brown in the sun
rise at the line's descending
where tide sands bloom
in a daily spring.
Where no bells ring,
suncast and moonspell
woo from their salty sleep
Diotima's dream
       diatoms
            (algae whose life is a single cell)

hearing without ears
in the gloom of their atoms
the voice of God, diurnal
        singing
splitting day from night
and in "Let there be light"
knowing signs as in seasons or days or years,
a meek creation metronomed
though blind.

Locked deep in the void of eyeless mind
swart sun begets a subtle day
and the moon's dark flight
perfects delight,
a thrill in organic clocks'
        uprising,
        downgliding,
(in pilgrims' old micrometry)
as in dampened deserts of Abraham's seed
eternity rocks
(light without sight)
(love's chambered night)
freighted and graced with rhythms—
        heartbeats
from a silent and sightless world.

Nighthawk River

Groping again
where pale and lucid drops,
sunlight on the bleak stones
unended rounding
touch of
moss in the gloom,
tufted like shrub, like
a beard of sponges, ashen
where ancient footfalls
lost to the light
still stir.

I hunt for your shadow,
Hawk of Night.

Reaching with fingers, bark over bone
where hidden rivers, quick and sweet,
slow under maps of riven skin,
where follicle and root grow cold
at forest's edge, and brow bends
lank as limbfall,
hair upon water.

Come, lithe current: smooth away
what still from light to light
leaps broken,
runs harrow-eyed and restless,

Yet rested here.
Here
in the stoop of sleep
the surface trembled once
shaped shadow with leaf and light;

striation and sinew here
once wrestled for life,
flexed till the lichen burst.

O still, small stream,
in taste of stone and ice
descend. Distill your name.

In your embrace I'll learn to drink
till teeth and lips and throat rejoice.

ב Beit

Still you were listening, discretely,
just when desire might, fractured, fold
under the weight of welcome: "Stay."
Yet what should keep me here? "Thought."
I, to hold the road and run
had sought some sort of pardon,
striven for goals, to bring some prize.
But nightfall and heartache all denied.

You opened a door on my broken pride,
said, "See, a hearth warms here for you.
Just open your hand, and close your eyes;
only in trust will your hope remain;
only for love will my peace come true.

"Come rest you from such foolish strife,
be home in a house not built with hands.
For you I wept in the falling dark.
For you on the path I lived and died."

Comfort in Imperfection

for Gideon

The smallest birds see colors not there
        for us, so biologists say
—the same or their ilk who used to teach
        that the animal view was deficiently grey,
their spectrum drab from black to white.

Media-clips of scientist-talk
        —assured, predictable, white-coat words—
say instruments gather what flesh can't prove;
        now by faith one infers spectrascopical birds
iridescently visioned past blue and pink.

And it may be as they think.

Yet the seasoned mind's eye looks up
        aloft where the eagle's drifting gaze
scans *us*, discretely reckoning.
        In the shy surmise of a tree-top thrush
glimmers light unknown, enough to amaze.

It's the common in thought we can trust:
        that like birds our light is broken through,
refracted into rainbow parts;
        that on earth we never see light true,
till changed in flight our sight comes new.

ג Gimel

Cramped in a corner, head to the wall;
Covering, cowering. Wounds like stones.
Thudding fear we walked through. Stopped.
Screaming silence. Every breath a bait
For the auld dodger.

I heard a clicking like knives in the August grass.
Too late this harvest for wonted feasting.
Creaking. The door jamb stuck.

I ask you:
What labor could admit,
What camel stoop so low,
What grass or flesh thread grow
To slip straight through the dry eye
And stitch it up? "Mend!" he said,
"I beg you, brother, mend!"

Cornered now, what's left to learn?
This struggling, like another siege at Troy,
Now ceased. To what pierced hand,
Huge, still holding out,
Or from what lips and tongue still blood wet
Could come the threading awl
To sew this darkness down?

Battered, I wait for a word.
Old mender of mind:
I plead for signs; my eyes are blind.
And yet I fear it: your Voice,
Answering. Just around the corner,
Time after time.

Dèserted

Bound to admit who chose the route
I pace it out. Yet the long drought
avails us little solace, and there are times
when I doubt ever to break the fast.

Fast to a desert course I keep
my broken-bridled horse, reins that tight
they and these hands are almost severed
with the strain. But not released.

Released from the burden of hollow time,
from the sorrow of dead tomorrows,
then could I gladly ride! Trusting to hope,
so turn to learn, unravel the secret—speak.

Speak to me then of love, whose welcome lines
stir life again, and rein me with that voice
whose patient calling bids me peace—
whose kind remembrance hymns release.

Lent

In this ash smudged
a cross; my brow aflame.
What seed has grown?

Or under those furrows,
skin and bone,
what fate foreknown,
what thought was sown?

"Dust you are," the old priest said,
"to dust you shall return."
Not bed, nor sleep, nor dream this night
but dirt and worms shall trace your plight
till ancient wrongs are set to right.

Sorrow.

Tomorrow is your kingdom shown:
ashes and dust
moth and rust
dirge for an empty home.

Solitary Dove, Easter Morning

in memoriam M.C.B.

What, dove, this Easter morning,
that you should sigh, low on the earth
beneath my window?
This cell looks out on light,
rays from rising solar fires
angled low through shining wreaths,
leaves of the yew tree where you rest,
ring-marked, grey robed,
greeting the sun.

This is the morning for all rejoicing:
the Son has risen. Yet your voice still
seems fraught, yearning, tinged with anticipation,
longing as though for another sun, another day.

Amen. Alone, like you this day
my senses too reach out—
where far (or maybe not so far) away
the air is charged with sighs
—nay, cries of anguish, rent
as the slow world spins on its altered axis,
cruel and carnal.

When shall this flesh, this web of death
at last be overcome? Like you then, too,
I sigh, cry:
Even so Lord Jesus come!
Surely, Christ, your Bride is won.

St. Barnabas Eve

The trees outside my window creak
—cicadas, grating their limbs
oblivious, a parody of settling birds
whose faded notes float far away.

Night ombres in, exhales its humid
breath into this court—a pledge;
the fragile tips of slated roofs
beyond blush pink with ebbing day.

The safer world vacates: in darkling
inconsistencies of mood I bide
the watch of evensong without—
within no solace but to pray.

Of one whose Word prevenes my way
I beg for mercy, lest I stray.

Coin of the Realm

Once it was called deceit;
Now nothing is false
If it serves an advantage.
One excuses what one must.

After all, who could expect less
From the lips of those
Who have such power
And will not share their glory?

When Augustus Caesar saw necessity
He cut to the chase,
Minted his divinity on metal coins,
Asserted his prerogatives.

So shall it be over us
In the coming age,
When the Truth Exchange
Forbids every word not fiction.

Madonna del Libro (Botticelli)

for Dominic

"...*sicut ablactatus est super matre sua,
Ita retributio in anima mea.*" (Psalm 131:2)

Having calmed myself
by the music of comforting words,
I am quieted now, as the psalm said,
like a weaned child with its mother.
The soul that is within me
turns to that wise and loving face
intent on the Book before us, steadied on her knees.
I gently touch the words; they leap to life
as she reads them, kneads them, praying
"Let it be unto me according to thy word."

For me as well this word is good, but good too
that my eyes are not yet raised too high;
nor do I yet occupy myself
with things too great, too marvelous for me.

Ascending the hard steps shall come soon enough,
that passage as the first at cost of blood.
Words hidden now shall be revealed. More stark,
laid bare in tightening coils of thorny consequence.

Child's Play and Painting

If I cannot see your face
how could you know my name?

But the sightless man was not a child.
His game was earnest: what he saw
he saw by sense and crafted speech.
Consider then his surprise.

All night long, year after year
he had waited in the dark.
Then the voice came, saying
Pardon this spittle and mud;
I mean it for your useless eyes.

Sealed with clay
                Ashes and dust
Sent to the water
                Washed in blood

Of course, he heard them—
cut lips curled, teeth set on edge
soured with ancestral grapes and stained

saying
                this man did sin and his parents too
                blind led the blind

saying
> since we can plainly see your face
> why shouldn't you know our names?

Sealed with clay
> *Ashes and dust*

Sent to the water
> *Washed in blood*

Then making it clear in the dust, one finger, painting.
Blind, you might have seen—
insisting sight your speech is spleen
perverse, unteachable; it shames.

> The rest is miracle.
> What you can tell remains.

ד Dalit

As rivers in flood run down to the sea
So my soul, Lord, to bless thee
Flows
Verdant with leaves blown free—
Wrested from doubt—
Glides now toward this mouth,
Slow-scape from a fecund heart.

A wider scape awaits:
In nearshore sea birds' flight
Unfurled,
Peace in the tidesong, sprung,
Rung from an unseen shore—
Choirs of musings, gleaming like fish,
Whirl bright in the morning sun.

Mary of Bethany, in Later Life

for Dorothy

*"So teach us to count our days,
That we may gain a wise heart." (Psalm 90:12)*

When morning sun sifts through the trees
my heart remembers you my God,
in mist-suffusèd light my knees
press earth which you yourself have trod.

Your faithful love, your promise sure
fills up my waking heart with joy;
let my forgetful thought grow pure,
that mindful cares might not alloy

the gold which you have dearly wrought
from dross and refuse of my days,
refined in me, that what Love bought
by sacrifice supreme may praise

the Lover of my soul in bliss,
not sparing to repay in kind,
enamored by that holy kiss
may linger close, time out of mind.

Musqueam Park

Tree light, sylvan storied
dappling down each shadow's dancing
patterning the forest floor:
here we, light leaved,
stand under, traces in a book.

As drawn to the wood we look.
Have we seen your glory, Lord?
Longing to go deeper in the silence
springing, now we gambol
greeny in the laughter of your gentle play,
full of the joy of earth's dim gleaming.

Thus we are made, not making,
written, not writing upon;
quieted in waiting, our rest disclosed,
hidden in weavings of your looming Word.

Heart under bark, still beating,
recall our shadowed thoughts, our tears—
with tender radiance streaming, speak!
Be heard!
in us, o Lord, be brightly heard.

Nechamu נַחֲמוּ

on Isaiah 40:1

The word is comfort. Second person plural,
Imperative verb. Not to be misunderstood.
It doesn't mean 'relax' or, 'take it easy someplace rural',
But implies instead a future city one could
Just about imagine, and though far off, still
Guaranteed, a promise yet to be fulfilled.

In time, in this terrestrial space
All flesh shall, trembling, see the Lord.
His captive chosen, those who face
Again a long exile, here heard a word
Not just for them but for their seed,
A remnant who the final Word will heed.

Finding solace in a future good meant
Not for now but generations yet to come
Requires more than faith; inspired love sent
Out to those unborn prompts hope for some
Whose faces we can't see, indeed, for Jews
Who Abram saw far off, but God alone did choose.

Semiotic

for S.W., in Advent

The babble of our many tongues
drowns out the dream of common meaning;
we climb alone on slippery rungs,
our scale of reason fogged and leaning
to no solid rock or wall.
We stammer, stutter, stumble, fall.

When Jacob dreamt he wondered there
at angels climbing up and down,
in silence at Beth-el. His share
of meaning came as gift, renown
by which a Hebrew word can bear
a seed of meaning voiced elsewhere.

But still, those angels did not speak,
as once to Abram, then to others would
in Hebrew, Aramaic, Parsi, Greek.
Those messengers were better understood.
Such also was the speech at Shavuot,
tongues of men and angels, polyglot.

Did all these speak the ur-language of God?
Or mere translations? More like that, it seems.
Who now as then would reck his rod

may gather but what judgment deems
imperfect, something overheard—
adaptable philology.

Yet words are deeds and deeds are word,
Semeia, seeds, signs in the old theology,
grace notes for the listening heart which wakes
to the *arché* of the universe, so takes
the Word made flesh to be God's own;
better than messengers: Seed to perfection sown.

Future Perfect

for Fr. T.V.

"With clouds descending," says the book,
the day of his appearing, thus,
might, just as any other, look
at first like when from broken skies to us
a sudden ray of sun shines through,
greening the ground on which we stand.

Some dissent. In these dark times new
wording twists; others demand
no word be true, this or its opposite.
We lack firm footing, definitions,
seeking to mean, not sure of it,
fearing to own our premonitions.

Yet wisdom, built on the Rock, relates
incipit to *explicit,* still yields
a universe proved finite, anticipates
the coming quantum shift, a paradox revealed
as Alpha and Omega, the cosmic plan
at last concluded, God with man
        forever.

Evensong: on Praying the Psalms

Your words breathe, their sound like leaves
burning in the autumn wind
kissed by the light to flame
of a thousand perfect candles.

Our words halt, one dim glow
in the teeming dark. Caves
writhing with images too scree
or stark to warrant trust

sap strength by which to make the leap
so longed for—spark into light,
that darkness might be washed away
where all is rest, and more than words.

You, our steadfast, ancient love,
in dream, in sleep, pray ever speak.

*"All mankind is of one author, and is one volume;
when one man dies, one chapter is not torn out of the book,
but translated into a better language,
and every chapter must be so translated. . . .
God's hand is in every translation,
and his hand shall bind up all our scattered leaves again
for that library where every book shall lie open to one another."*

(John Donne, *Devotions upon Emergent Occasions*,
Meditation XVII)

www.ingramcontent.com/pod-product-compliance
Lightning Source LLC
Chambersburg PA
CBHW071131090426
42736CB00012B/2083